# The Discipleship Series

## Other titles in the series

# 9
# Steps to a Renewed Life

Published by CWR, Waverley Abbey House,
Waverley Lane, Farnham, Surrey GU9 8EP, England.

Copyright © 2002 by Selwyn Hughes.
First published in Great Britain 1979 as *Every Day with Jesus,*
*The Transformed Life,* January/February 1979
This revised edition 2002.

Front cover image: Helen Reason.
Images: Helen Reason.

Unless otherwise indicated, all Scripture references are from the Holy Bible:
*New International Version (NIV),* copyright © 1973, 1978, 1984 by the
International Bible Society.

Other Scripture quotations are marked:
Moffatt: *The Moffatt Translation of the Bible,* © 1987, Hodder & Stoughton
NKJ: *New King James Version,* © 1982, Thomas Nelson Inc.
TLB: *The Living Bible,* © 1971, 1994, Tyndale House Publishers

ISBN 1 85345 220 3

Concept development, editing, design and production by CWR.

Typesetting: David Andrew Design.
Printed: Omnia Books Ltd.

# 9

# Steps to a Renewed Life

Selwyn Hughes

# Contents

# Introduction

*"For as he thinks in his heart, so is he." (Proverbs 23:7, NKJ)*

Every one of us, from the moment we are born to the moment we die, undergo a continual process of transformation and change. It is not a question of whether we wish it or not, for the process is largely inevitable. Hour by hour, day by day and year by year, we are being changed – for better or worse. The forces and pressures of life that surround us transform us into a certain pattern. We stand in the midst of these life forces as free agents and, by the power of choice, we decide the pattern. Even in deciding nothing, allowing life to flow over and around us, our very indecision is a decision: not to decide.

On London's Embankment, many years ago, I talked to a dirty and dishevelled tramp who greatly surprised me by taking out of his pocket a worn and faded photograph of a handsome barrister. "This was me," he said, "before I discovered that my partner had been embezzling our financial resources." He went on to tell me that the shock of the discovery had driven him to drink and ultimately to the pitiable plight of a London tramp. Regrettably, the man had been transformed into the image of his decisions. The hurt started off a chain reaction of conflicts that left him a human wreck. Had he reacted rightly to the blow he could have turned the setback into a springboard, but the wrong reaction let in the forces of disruption and decay, which plunged him into the abyss of human failure. When we allow ourselves to get into a conflict, we soon become a conflict and end up looking like a conflict. Nothing can be sadder.

The thesis of this title in the "Discipleship" series is quite simple: every one of us is constantly undergoing a process of change – for better or worse. So inevitable is this change that someone once said of it, "There is nothing changeless about life – except change itself." One writer claims, "The science of semantics [i.e. the meaning of words] is based on the fact that human nature is changing every moment. So, when you use a word to describe a man, you must define which man – the man a year ago, the man a month ago, the man a week ago, or the man *now*. You must, therefore, change your words to describe the changed man." It must be carefully noted, however, that this inevitable change, which runs through life, can transform us not only into lower patterns but also into higher ones. But only if we choose it. We can decide which forces we will allow to shape and mould us. The great writer, Henry F. Lyte, when penning the words, "Change and decay in all around I see", expressed only a half-truth, for it is possible to allow the forces that flow from Jesus Christ to so operate within us that change and decay become instead change and transformation. The fact is that when men and women mentally shut the door to Jesus Christ and the upward thrust He gives to life, they open the door to change in a downward direction. Only those forces which we allow to affect us do affect us. It is possible to allow the power that resides in Jesus Christ to work in you so that you can become a transformed person – transformed upwards.

My prayer is that you will experience the life-transforming power found only in Christ as you embark on one of the most exciting and, possibly, most life-changing journeys of your life.

# 1

# Right
# **decisions**

*"When we are willing to lay the blame for our moral plight squarely on ourselves then transformation can begin."*

From the moment of birth to the moment of death, transformation and change are inevitable. As we are transformed into the image of our decisions and, as we have said, it is only those forces which we allow to affect us that do affect us, this places a great responsibility upon each one of us to make the right decisions and choices. Some will counter this by saying that it isn't quite as easy as that, for there are other factors in the universe that make the possibility of upward transformation seem highly questionable. They will present such things as heredity, circumstances, the presence of evil, being born under a bad star, the subconscious and environmental conditioning. These, they claim, greatly affect our ability to choose and, therefore, man is a creature more sinned against than sinning. When anything goes wrong in life, our first impulse is to blame someone else and look around for some way of evading responsibility. This device of human nature is, of course, as old as

Adam who said, "The woman you put here with me – she gave me some fruit from the tree, and I ate it" (Gen. 3:12). Most people blame God for the plight of mankind. "If God is all-powerful," they say, "why didn't He make a world that couldn't go wrong?" This is neither the place nor the time to answer that question except to say that blaming our predicament on God doesn't get us out of it. "Evasions don't evade, excuses don't excuse, dodging doesn't dodge, except propel us into deeper problems."

## The choice is always ours

*What are some of the alleyways into which people run to evade responsibility?* When a Muslim gets into difficulty he blames his kismet – his fate. But as he believes his kismet is ordained by God he is indirectly making God responsible. When a Hindu or a Buddhist gets into trouble, he blames his karma – the result of the deeds of a previous birth now catching up with him. An authority on Indian customs says of this approach to life, "He removes the responsibility from the 'now' to the 'then' and to a person of whom he has no memory. It saves him from the necessity of finding the cause in his present actions and attitudes." Here, in the West, people evade their responsibility in many ingenious ways. Some blame the stars. As if worlds spinning in outer space could affect the destiny of free moral agents! Others blame the subconscious and claim that the drives which go in there are, in a large measure, out of our control. Still others blame the environment and claim that man is just an animal in a cage and that all his actions result from an attempt to adapt to his environment.

Another way in which people try to evade responsibility is to say that we are only doing what everyone else does – so laying the blame on the behaviour of others. How absurd! There is only one way out and that is to lay the blame where it belongs – on ourselves. It is not so much what happens to us but how we respond to it that matters. And the choice is *always ours*.

# The divided self

Humanity, in general, and under one guise or another, seeks to evade responsibility for what it is and we must now examine an evasion more subtle than the others. The problem is presented thus: "Nothing can be done for me because, although I accept the responsibility for what I am, there are really two persons inside me, one striving to be good and the other striving to be bad. And the bad is too strong for me. I'm not affected by outside forces, I'm beaten by myself!" The poet Browning expressed this divided condition in these words:

Sadly mixed natures; self-indulgent, yet
Self-sacrificing too: how the love soars,
How the craft, avarice, vanity and spite
Sink again!

This condition of the divided self is extremely sad, but not hopeless. Paul's words, "O wretched man that I am! Who will deliver me ... I thank God – through Jesus Christ our Lord!" (Rom. 7:24–25, NKJ), are viewed in two ways by Bible scholars. Some say the words express his feelings prior to his conversion, while others say that they are the expression of his feelings after conversion, in which he describes the conflict between the new nature (in Christ) and the carnal nature. Whichever view you take, the important thing to see is that he discovered the answer to his problem in the next chapter – and that is Christ. Jesus solved Paul's dilemma and He can solve yours. The Everlasting Mercy in pursuing you has set up a war within your soul. But the pangs you feel are His prods – prodding you to be a transformed person.

# How it begins

It is time now to come to a definite conclusion, and our conclusion is this: when we are willing to lay the blame for our moral plight squarely on ourselves then transformation can begin.

When a man or woman stands up and says, "I am responsible for the kind of person I am. I am what I wanted to be. Now I've changed my mind. I'm sorry for what I have done. I'm going to ask God's forgiveness and the forgiveness of any I have hurt on the way up through life and, with His love and grace flowing through me, I shall be different", then they will discover that a miracle is about to begin. I say "about to begin" because transformation (in the Christian sense of the word) takes place when words become the true expression of the feelings. It is not enough to merely say it, it must be said vitally – with the whole person behind it. When you stop being a puppet (someone pushed around by pressures and problems from the past) and become a person who accepts the responsibility of making a sound decision – then you are at the point of transformation, which the Bible calls conversion. The first step in becoming a Christian is to accept the responsibility of making a decision that you, and only you, can make. No one can make it for you – not even God Himself. You admit that you are a sinner and that you are responsible for the way you have gone. As you do this, then put your life, just as it is, into God's hands through His Son, Jesus Christ, you will discover that the power of God will be released into your life and the transformation upwards will begin.

## Partnership with God

As we come to the end of this first step towards a transformed life, we pause to clarify what conversion really is. It is a fundamental change, by which a person passes from the kingdom of self into the kingdom of God. It is variously described in the New Testament as conversion, new birth, new creation, being made partakers of the divine nature, alive to God or being transformed. The richest phrases in the human language have been seized upon in an effort to describe this most important thing that can happen to a human being. There are two major invisible forces that affect our lives, one is the force of sin and evil that seeks to drag us downwards. The other is the force of God's goodness which seeks to draw us upwards. We stand at the centre of these forces which seek to influence us mainly through our wills. We can decide to be transformed from above or from below. When conversion does take place (and I sincerely hope it has happened to you) and you pass out of the sphere of the kingdom of self and enter the sphere of the kingdom of God, you change worlds, and between those two worlds is the difference between hell and heaven. Here, in this new sphere of living, you and God work out life *together*. You and God become partners; God, the senior partner and you, the managing director. With God as your Father and Jesus Christ as your Saviour, then life takes on new power, new direction, new goals, new vitality, new adequacy. You are a transformed person.

# 2

# **Freedom**
# from self

*"Whatever gets your attention gets you."*

We saw, in the last chapter, that all of life is based on transformation. A doctor writing on this point put it this way:

> We take air into our lungs and transform the blood from impure to pure, and send it on its healing, life-sustaining way; we take in food and transform it into blood and tissue and cell; we transform mere sense impressions upon the retina into sight; we take wild sounds and tame them to time and tune and make them into music; we take two people, tie them together with bonds of love and make them into a family, we take the self-centred soul, get him to surrender to Christ and he is transformed, not only into a living soul, but into a life-giving spirit.

Now that we have established that transformation upwards commences with conversion, we must move on to examine how it is continued. The answer is in 2 Corinthians 3:18:

> And we, who with unveiled faces all reflect the Lord's glory, are being transformed into his likeness with ever-increasing glory, which comes from the Lord, who is the Spirit.

"We, who with unveiled faces ... are being transformed into his likeness." Can you see the breathtaking thought contained in these thrilling words? This is what the apostle is saying: As we stand before the Person of our Lord, and continuously gaze upon His Face, we are gradually changed into His likeness, and we proceed from one degree of glory to another. The Holy Spirit within us is the silent Artist who captures the glory and radiance of Christ, and imprints it upon our own individual characters and personalities. Gazing upon Him we become like Him.

> That one dear Face, far from vanishing rather grows ...
> Becomes my universe that feels and knows.

## The laws of our personality

Someone has called this "the most profound thought in all the Scriptures" – that simply by gazing upon Christ we become like Him. We now ask ourselves a question. *Why is it that the New Testament lays such stress on the need to constantly focus on Christ?* The answer is quite simple – it frees us from self-preoccupation. All the cults emphasise the need to look at oneself. "Discover the divine within you," they say, "and you will rise to new heights of self-discovery." If you follow this advice then you will end up being preoccupied with your own state of mind and emotion. Hebrews 12:2 gets our gaze focused in the right direction – Christward: "Keep your eyes on Jesus, our leader and instructor. He was willing to die a shameful death on the cross because of the joy he knew would be his afterwards ..." (TLB). One of the great laws of human personality is this: *whatever gets your attention gets you.* This insight goes like a dart to the heart of our problem. If Christ gets our attention then He gets us – fully and completely. God is not only concerned in saving us from sin; He is equally concerned in saving us from ourselves, and focusing our attention on Christ provides us with the means by which this can be achieved. Another law of human personality states: *we become like the object on which we focus*. People who are interested in nothing, begin to look like the object of their attention and have a look of blankness about their expression and their personalities become a blur. If our gaze is focused solely on ourselves, then we become depressed. If it is focused on others, we become distressed. But if it is focused fully on Christ, then we become delighted.

## Picked to pieces

Years ago I received a letter from a lady which adds great weight to what we are saying. She wrote, "I have spent years undergoing psychoanalysis and, after spending hundreds of pounds on this method of therapy, I am no better." She is not the first person I have come across who, having been psychoanalysed, was left more disrupted than ever. Some benefit from it, of course, and it would be wrong to suggest that it has no positive results, but its main weakness is that, when practised outside of a Christian context, it leaves you centred on yourself. Since secular psychiatry doesn't know how to get people beyond themselves to God, it leaves them preoccupied with techniques and procedures. It picks them to pieces and doesn't know how to put them together again. Here, of course, Christianity steps in and shows that the way to health is through self-surrender to God. If God is left out then what else is there on which to centre? The patient's own self or the analyst. Anything that leaves you centred on yourself or on something less than God, leaves you off-centre – for you are not God. The whole thrust of the Christian message is first to move the human spirit off its idolatrous centre, self, to revolve around its proper centre, God, and then to hold it there by the constant focusing of the spirit on Jesus Christ. Self, in our own hands, is a problem and a pain. In God's hands it becomes a possibility and a progression.

## "Time exposure to God"

The law of self-surrender is the first law of life. To surrender to God can be humbling to the human ego and, therefore, many try to skirt around the necessity. All they succeed in doing, however, is to trip over an unsurrendered ego into a life of unhappiness and frustration. The centre of all sin is self-centredness. Halford Luccock has defined sin as "disharmony with the moral nature and purpose of God as revealed in Christ". To be centred on self is to attempt to arrange the universe around a wrong centre. Conversion is the act by which God removes us from a self-centre to a God-centre. Once we become Christians, however, we discover that the law which brought us to conversion is the same one that sustains us in it. We focus on Christ for conversion and we must also focus on Him for continuance.

Set your minds on things above, not on earthly things. For you died, and your life is now hidden with Christ in God. (Col.3:2–3)

We now ask ourselves: *What are some of the ways in which we Christians can keep our gaze fully focused on Christ?* We can do it firstly by ensuring that we set up a daily Quiet Time. The Quiet Time is a period of just gazing at the face of Christ. Prayer has been defined as "time exposure to God". As you focus on Christ in your daily time with Him, you will become like that on which you gaze. You are made one degree more Christ-like every moment you spend with Him. The Quiet Time produces the quiet heart. You realise, as you wait before Him, that the One into whose face you gaze has the last word in human affairs. Beholding Him everything within you is drawn to health. You leave the Quiet Time feeling refreshed, renewed, *whole*.

## We love – "because"

I want to emphasise the point that the Christian life rises and falls at the point of the devotional. Prayer and the study of the Scriptures are of the utmost importance, but each one of us needs a few moments during the day when we take time to express our love to the Lord Jesus Christ and cultivate a rich romantic relationship with Him. How is this done? How do we learn the art of deepening our love for Him? By focusing on the fact of His love for us. The love that underlies all effective Christian living and service is not one that is manufactured but borrowed. We gaze upon Him, let His love pour through into our spirits and, slowly but surely, the machinery of our soul whirrs into activity, so that we go out to love as He loves, think as He thinks and serve as He serves. When Christians say to me, "How can I love Christ more?" I usually respond by saying, "You are focusing in the wrong direction. Concentrate on how much He loves you and you will never again need to ask that question." The secret of Christian love is caught up in these immortal words, "We love ... because He first loved us" (1 John 4:19, NKJ). Notice what it says: "We love ... because ..." In other words, *it is His love which is the reason for ours.* In focusing on Christ in our daily Quiet Time, we open the inner sluice gates of our soul and the ocean of His love pours in. All service and activity then rises like a raft to fulfil His purposes. We discover, when this happens, that we are not working to earn His approval, but working because we have it. And the difference is crucial.

## Shut in with God

"Those who do not provide for a Quiet Time, preferably in the early morning before the day begins," said a well-known missionary, "will provide for an unquiet time throughout the day." If you do not start right, the probabilities are that you will have to take some time to yourself for medication, relaxation, regret, frustration or repentance. Imagine a diver too busy to think about getting his breathing apparatus in working order before he descends into the depths. He would be no more foolish than the Christian who descends into the stifling atmosphere of today's world without getting his breathing apparatus of prayer and meditation connected with the pure air of the kingdom of God. A traveller passing through the Panama Canal wrote, "Our ship moved into the lock. The great sea gates were closed upon us. We, who had sailed the oceans, were blocked, shut in, helpless, our freedom gone. But lo, we felt a great lifting, great fountains were opened from beneath, and to our astonishment, the great ship was lifted thirty-five feet in just seven minutes. Then the gates opened and we glided out on a higher level on to the bosom of Lake Gatún." The Quiet Time does that – it shuts you in with God and for a while it seems that nothing happens. Then, however, infinite resources begin to bubble up, and you are lifted silently, powerfully, without noise or strain, onto a higher level. The gate opens and you move out to experience a higher level of life. You wonder, and so do others, how you can cope with the problems and the worries. The secret is simple. It's the result of having been shut in with God.

## Quiet or unquiet?

As we said, those who miss out on a Quiet Time finish up with an unquiet time. Pascal said, "Nearly all the ills of life spring from this simple source, that we are not able to sit still in a room." The Quiet Time offers more than sitting still; in the stillness we can meet with God. A Christian author tells how, in a time of deep spiritual need, she watched the sun rise over the Grand Canyon in Arizona, USA: "The sun began to rise, flashing its glory light upon the heavens above, making them look like the divine painter's palette; then gradually touching one point after another in the Canyon and lighting it into gorgeous colouring." She then explains how, through the whole day, she drank in the scene until darkness fell and then it was gone. "But not," she goes on to say, "not gone forever. It was imprinted on my mind to remain there the rest of my life." This is what the Quiet Time will do for you. You get up early as the sun rises and you take a "time exposure" to God. It is printed indelibly upon you. And, when the sun sets, the vision is still there – within you.

# 3

# Transformation
## through God's initiative

*"To be transformed men and women, we do not have to try and find God, but simply let Him find us."*

We begin this chapter by asking ourselves a provocative question: *In this process of transformation, does God undergo a transformation in order to transform us?* If so then the possibility of our being transformed is divinely guaranteed. The staggering truth of the matter is that, in the mighty act of the incarnation, God has become like us in order that we might become like Him. "Is there anything more stupendous in the annals of history," wrote someone, "than God being transformed into our image in order that we might be transformed into His?" The incarnation is the miracle of miracles. Once we see it in this light then all other miracles in the New Testament become convincing and credible. The fact is described for us: "Though he was divine by nature, he did not set store upon equality with God, but emptied himself ..." (Phil. 2:6, Moffatt). This is not man becoming God, but God becoming man and becoming man at the point of his deepest need.

Alan W. Watts in his book, *Behold the Spirit*, says,

> The meaning of the Incarnation, therefore, is simply that we do not have to attain union with God. Man does not have to climb to the infinite and become God, because, out of love, the infinite God descends to the finite and becomes man. Once we realise the futility of our pride, that we can neither ascend to God, nor prevent his descent to us, the proud core of egoism is simply dissolved.

## Consent to be found

The incarnation is the most important truth in the Christian faith.

> This is how God showed his love among us: He sent his one and only Son into the world that we might live through him. This is love: not that we loved God, but that he loved us and sent his Son as an atoning sacrifice for our sins. (1 John 4:9–10)

If we miss this then we by-pass the centre and finish up on the outskirts of truth, lost, confused and bewildered. In order to be transformed men and women, we do not have to try and find God, but simply let Him find us. "Religion," someone said, "is man's search for God, the gospel is God's search for man. There are many religions, but only one gospel." Jesus is the personal approach from an unseen God, coming so near to us that to miss Him we deliberately have to run in the opposite direction. To discover God, then, is the easiest thing in the world. You don't have to struggle or strive – you simply have to consent to be found. No one is farther than one step from God. A friend of mine, a preacher of the gospel, when asked, "Can you tell me the way to heaven", replied, "Certainly. Turn right round and keep straight on."

There are two ways of reaching the house next door. One is to travel all the way around the globe; the other is to walk a few feet. There are two ways of finding transformation – one is to walk right around the globe making a concentrated effort to get rid of your faults and disciplining yourself into being worthy of God's interest and concern. An impossible task, of course. The other way is to step next door, say, "Yes," to Jesus Christ, and accept the gift of His salvation. Transformation is not something you attain – but obtain. You accept the gift, and then belong to the Giver.

## God's best photograph

God apparently is so convinced of our need to be completely transformed, that He has taken the extraordinary step of becoming a man, so that we might become like Him. This fact must be burned deeply into our minds so that we will give up our self-strivings and egocentric attempts at transformation, in favour of letting God find us and renew us. We don't have to ascend up to heaven to bring God down by our efforts. He's down. The incarnation brought Him to us.

The Son is the radiance of God's glory, and the exact representation of his being, sustaining all things by his powerful word. After he had provided purification for sins, he sat down at the right hand of the Majesty in heaven. (Heb. 1:3)

Quintin Hogg, in his younger days, gave his time and attention to some down-and-out boys in a poor part of London. One of the young men, a wild and wayward character before Quintin Hogg influenced him, was asked by a friend how he managed to keep going straight. "Oh," he said, "it's not too difficult. You see I always carry a photo of 'QH' and, when I am tempted, I just take it out and look at it. It helps me to overcome." In Christ we have the best photograph God ever took and, when tempted to go astray, we look at Him and see God.

Browning wrote:

'Tis the weakness in strength, that I cry for!
My flesh that I seek in the Godhead! I seek it and find it.
A Face like my face that receives thee; a Man like to me
Thou shalt love and be loved by, for ever: a Hand like this hand
Shall throw open the gates of new life to thee!
See the Christ stand!

## The divine initiative

The most beautiful verse in the whole of Scripture is John 3:16: *"For God so loved the world that he gave his one and only Son, that whoever believes in him shall not perish but have eternal life."* This verse confirms what we have been saying – God came down in infinite identification so that we might go up in infinite identification. Some years ago I had the privilege of addressing a large crowd of pilgrims and tourists gathered for the usual Sunday morning service outside the empty tomb at the foot of Gordon's Calvary in Jerusalem. Against the backdrop of the skull-shaped hill, I preached on this text and afterwards an American visitor said to me, "I have always considered John 3:16 to be so charged with new wine that one phrase from it leaves one intoxicated with redemption. To drink of it all, as we have done this morning has transformed me into another person." This matchless verse tells us that the initiative for our transformation begins with God. "For God so loved the world." All other religions begin "For man so eagerly sought for God that ...". Literature fairly bulges with accounts of men and women who, in attempting to find God, have stormed the throne of grace with clamorous and vociferous demands that the Almighty must respond, believing that God's calmness must be disturbed before He will hearken to their requests. The truth, however, is this: we do not have to overcome God's reluctance, but simply lay hold of His highest willingness. In coming to us, God took the initiative. "We love Him because he first loved us."

## God was in Christ

"God so loved the world that he gave his one and only Son." Surely this is the most beautiful description of the most beautiful fact that ever took place – that God allowed Himself to be transformed into our likeness so that we can be transformed into His. A missionary, speaking to a group in India about God's love for the world, asked his audience for their response to this exciting fact. A village woman spoke up and said, "What kind of Father was He to send His Son – why didn't He come Himself?" It was a deep and penetrating question, but the missionary was able to explain that God was present in the Person of His Son and that when we take hold of Christ we take hold of the very nature and character of God.

"I love Jesus, but I dislike God," said a little girl, "for God wanted to destroy the world, but Jesus wouldn't let Him." She saw Jesus as a third person standing between herself and God – a mistake that countless thousands of adults make. Jesus is a mediator only in the sense that He mediates God to us, for "God was reconciling the world to himself in Christ" (2 Cor. 5:19). A true Christian is not able to tell where Jesus ends and where God begins in his experience; they melt into one. When he deepens his consciousness of God then he deepens, at the same time, his Christ-consciousness. When he deepens his Christ-consciousness, he deepens His God-consciousness. God and Christ are not rivals. They do not push each other out of the way. They are one – in nature, in character and in purpose.

## The width of God's love

So how wide is God's redemption? John 3:16 uses a word that is one of the most exciting in the whole of the Scriptures: "whoever". It is a word that stretches its arms across the five continents and the seven seas. It knows no limit and leaps over all barriers of class, colour and creed. Celsus, an early opponent of Christianity, objected to this aspect of Christianity, saying, "Other religions invite the respectable, the moral, the upright, but this faith scandalously invites the riff-raff, the immoral, the drunken, the dishonest – and welcomes them!" Thank God it does! But the riff-raff become the respectable, the immoral become moral and the drunken become sober. Some years ago, in a children's service, I tried a little experiment. I placed a coin underneath a cup and said, "Now whoever will come and take this coin can have it." Immediately a few dozen children rushed forward. "Now wait a minute," I said, "I don't remember inviting all you children to come out here." Nonplussed, they returned to their seats, except one brave boy who stood before the upturned cup. "What do you want?" I asked, looking suitably stern and serious.

"The money, sir," he said.

"I don't remember mentioning your name," I replied.

"No sir," he blurted out, "but you said 'whoever' – and that means me."

## "A thousand ages in the heart"

The last phrase in the verse we are focusing on is, "but have everlasting life". Some translations use the word "eternal" here; but the Greek word aionos carries two thoughts – "eternal" meaning quality of life, and "everlasting" meaning endless duration. It is, in other words, a quality of life which is everlasting because it cannot be confined to time. One preacher says of this phrase, "It bursts the seams of time as a butterfly bursts its chrysalis. It is so good, it just has to be eternal." A Harvard professor lectured on the question "Is Eternal Existence Desirable?" The conclusion he came to was that it is not. We cannot help but agree, for if eternity is just eternal existence then who desires it? But if it's eternal life – that's different. Life has to be eternal or else it is not really life. It has the seeds of death in it. George Bernard Shaw wrote, "I don't want to have to live with George Bernard Shaw for ever." If a person hates himself, then the thought of living forever with that self is no joke. But suppose you have a self with whom you can get along – a transformed self, a self you can respect and love in God, with the possibilities of even greater transformation – then that's different. Yes, eternal life has to be everlasting in quantity when it is eternal in quality. Chesterton said of Robert Louis Stevenson that he "died with a thousand stories in his heart". A Christian, when he dies has a thousand ages in his heart. The life of God within our hearts is so positively exhilarating that it has to be eternal. Nothing this good can ever end.

# 4

# Removing
the **veil**

*"We have to lift our veils if we wish to be transformed."*

We saw, in the last chapter, that God has taken the initiative in this great question of transformation, by first transforming Himself into our likeness so that we can be transformed into His. When Jesus was crucified, we read that, "the veil of the temple was torn in two" (Matt. 27:51, NKJ). Why was this? It was a solemn symbol of the fact that, in Christ, the heart of God is laid bare and God shows Himself as He really is – redemptive Love. Since God has unveiled Himself in Jesus, what then is our response? We, too, must unveil our faces, drop our masks, gaze upon Him in wonder and, in the gazing, we are made like Him. We are going to examine together the one central condition which will enable us to become more like Jesus Christ – "the unveiled face". We have to lift our veils if we wish to be transformed. The moment we do wrong or violate any spiritual principle, a veil immediately drops over our spirits. But the dropping of that veil is no solution, for the veil that shuts God out is the same veil that shuts us in, and to be shut in with a self that you cannot respect and love is to carry a living hell within. As we focus our spirits upon God and His Son, Jesus Christ, and lift the veil that hinders our gaze of Him, we are, by that continuous gazing, changed into Christ's glorious image. So we must lift our veils and learn to be open and honest with God. It may hurt our pride to do this, but if we are to experience spiritual, psychological and physical health it must be done. The Japanese, in dealing with pride, say they follow the onion skin method – peeling off layer after layer with tears.

## The unveiled face

One of the veils which we must lift off if we are to be transformed into the same image of Jesus, is the veil that lay upon the hearts of the Jews when Moses was read – *the veil of legalism.* "Even to this day when Moses is read, a veil covers their hearts" (2 Cor. 3:15). It is the belief that salvation is gained by what one does, rather than being something that Christ accomplishes in us and through us. Many come into the Christian life firmly renouncing self and letting Christ into the centre of their lives, but then promptly trying to live out the Christian life by self-effort and self-achievement. Self-centredness moves out at the moment of conversion, then creeps back to make its presence known at a later stage. When this happens then the Christian life is being lived out on the basis of self – *you* are doing it. Of course you call on Christ to help you in what you do, but that is using Christ rather than letting Him use you. The "unveiled face" means that, in continuous surrender, you transfer the centre from yourself to Christ. His love touches the springs of love within you, and you love in return. You can say with the little boy who said to his father, "Daddy, I love you and I'm going to do something about it." So your daily prayer becomes, "Jesus I love you and I'm going to do something about it." Your doing springs out of the loving, and the loving springs out of surrender. How sad it is to see Christians struggling to live out the Christian life in an act of self-effort. They are inwardly fighting and struggling – forcing themselves towards goodness. The Christian life is not you using Christ, but Christ using you.

## The veil of fear

Another veil that prevents the beauty and loveliness of Christ from breaking through into our personalities is *the veil of fear*. If we are to become like Christ then we must take steps to remove this veil from our spirits as quickly as possible. The best way to deal with fear is to first look at Christ fully in the face, then look our fears fully in the face. The order in which this is done is important. Gazing upon Christ helps us to transform our fears, for it centres our attention on the One who is the Master of the universe and the Controller of all our destinies.

> There is no fear in love. But perfect love drives out fear, because fear has to do with punishment. The one who fears is not made perfect in love. (1 John 4:18)

Luther once wrote to Melanchthon: "I am against those worries and fears which take the heart out of you. Why make God a liar in not believing His wonderful promises when He commands us to be of good cheer, and cast all our care upon Him? What more can the devil do than slay us? Why worry then since Christ is at the helm?" Ponder those words, "What more can the devil do than slay us?" There is infinite wisdom in that statement. One famous psychologist said, "Think of the worst that can possibly happen, face it in your mind, then relax." La Rochefoucald once said, "It is a sort of happiness to know the worst that can befall us. Man can stand anything when he knows everything. It is uncertainty that breaks us." As we focus our gaze fully upon Jesus, and learn that He has our lives fully in His hands, then we can turn to our fears, look them fully in the face, and say, "The worst that can happen is for you to throw me further into the arms of God." When fear knocks at your door learn to let Christ answer. It will soon run away.

## The veil of resentment

We now need to look at another veil that must be taken down if Christ's likeness is to be imprinted on our characters – *the veil of inner resentment and bitterness.* This, if it is not transformed, will transform us – into sour, morose and embittered souls.

Bear with each other and forgive whatever grievances you may have against one another. Forgive as the Lord forgave you. (Col 3:13)

A man, a very able minister of the gospel, once said to me, "I was taught a great deal in my training for the ministry, but no one ever taught me how to get rid of my resentments. Can you help me in this matter?" I looked into his face and saw in his countenance how bitterness and resentment were draining him spiritually, mentally and physically. No one, no matter how hard they try, can carry Christ's character in theirs when the veil of resentment hangs over their spirit. In one of the first churches I pastored, a deacon I greatly loved refused to give up his resentments. I talked to him about them, and said, "If you don't, then they will eventually kill you." This is exactly what did happen. In a deacons' meeting he got up to voice his disagreement over a certain issue – and dropped dead.

You can't properly focus on Christ if you hold resentment in your heart, for all your thoughts are pulled off on a tangent – pulled from the vertical to the horizontal by that resentment. Bitterness, hatred and resentment are self-defeating. There is only one way to overcome them. Gaze on Jesus and see what He did with all those people who could have caused Him to hate. He forgave them.

## The veil of impure thinking

No one need be ashamed of wrong or impure thoughts that leap unbidden into the mind, but another veil that must be removed if we are to be transformed into the same image as Jesus is *the veil of impure thinking*. A picture, a word, a story, an advertisement, a glance, an odour – almost anything can summon the thought. "Victory or defeat," said the late Dr W.E. Sangster, "turns on the skill and the speed by which the thought is managed in the mind." If a man turns his thoughts swiftly to spiritual things and focuses his gaze instantly on Christ, those evil thoughts can be outwitted and overcome. If, on the other hand, a person toys with the thought, allows the imagination to wallow in it, fondles it, harbours it and entertains it, instead of blasting it with prayer, then lust will soon take control, and anything can happen. One Christian view of morality is this – a man can keep the Ten Commandments and still be morally impure if he allows the central citadel of his mind to become preoccupied with impure thoughts. Let me make the point again – the thoughts that crowd unbidden into our minds are not sin. They become sin only when they are nurtured, fondled and entertained. To live, therefore, behind the veil of harboured impure thinking is to live in an inner hell of disloyalty, where one's self-respect is cancelled out by self-contempt. When, however, we gaze upon Christ with an unveiled face, His purity, so white and burning, is more than a match for the evil and impure thought which cannot stand the sight of Jesus and leaves the mind beaten and ashamed.

## A veil of excessive grief

Grief comes to us all. It is part of our human existence, from which nobody escapes. Yet some Christians prevent the beauty of Christ from spreading through their characters by holding *the veil of excessive grief* over their spirits. Whenever a calamity or the death of a loved one takes place then a certain amount of grief is natural and proper. Jesus wept at the grave of a loved one (John 11:35). Someone said that the greatest test of growth in Christian living is the measurement of the time which a person takes to get over grief. How are we to meet grief and sorrow? Firstly, by making up our minds that grief is bound to come. This attitude will save us from feeling, when it does come, that we are being singled out for persecution. If we don't prepare for it in this way, then we get drawn into what is known as a "persecution illusion" – or a martyr's complex. Illusions turn out, in the end, to be worse than realities. Do what Jesus did: "They rose up, put him out of the town, and brought him to the brow of the hill on which the town was built, in order to hurl him down. But he made his way through" (Luke 4:29–30, Moffatt). When faced with a problem he didn't back off or try to dodge the issue or even escape – He went straight through. The Christian word is "through". It faces everything and transforms everything.

Secondly, surrender your grief to God and spend more time than ever before in fellowship with Him. Pray not just for yourself but for others, because prayer for yourself does not cancel out loneliness. It may even aggravate it if you think only of yourself. Bring the needs of others into your life. This truly works.

## The veil of an uncleared conscience

The last veil which we allow to descend upon our spirits is the veil of *an uncleared conscience*. The moment we violate one of God's spiritual or moral principles then we immediately drop a veil, so that no one will know. It is the unconscious tribute we pay to goodness and God's moral laws. But the dropping of the veil produces only inner guilt, so we must learn to lift that veil by being honest with God, honest with ourselves and honest with others. No one gets away with anything in this universe, as Luke 12:2 clearly affirms: "Nothing is hidden that shall not be revealed, or concealed that shall not be made known." Violations will have to be revealed voluntarily and forgiveness sought, or else it will be "revealed" as an inner conflict, a complex, functional disease or personality disorder. Whenever we offend against God's principles then a curtain of guilt descends on our spirits. Remember, this feeling of guilt is redemptive. It is to the soul what pain is to the body. It is God's warning sign that something is wrong and attention must be paid to it. Psychologists and psychiatrists, who take the attitude that guilt (real guilt) is dangerous to the personality, and that conscience and morality are simply concepts, do more damage than they realise. They run counter to the laws of the universe. Guilt cannot be got rid of by ignoring it, laughing at it or dismissing it with a wave of the hand. God has arranged the universe so that we can only be comfortable in that which is good for us – His will. So every sin must be brought to Him for forgiveness, for only as that veil is lifted can He imprint His loveliness on our hearts.

# 5

# Right
# **thinking**

*"When your mind and God's mind come together, then everything, both in heaven and earth, fall into place."*

A great deal is said on the subject of right thinking. "Change your thinking," we are told "and you will change your personality." Books, magazines and newspapers pour out a steady stream of articles and features on this subject, yet, as someone has pointed out, "all this emphasis on salvation by thinking has served only to leave us with more disrupted people than ever".

The reason is quite simple – you cannot bring about any great changes in the mind until first there has been a change in the spirit. Our spirit is the motivating centre of our personality – the part which God specifically reserves for Himself and until He inhabits it and dwells in it, then it cannot be said of us that we are properly integrated persons. Once we surrender our spirits to God and allow Him to come in and take up His rightful abode, the process of central integration begins. Without God at the centre, trying to hold life together through the mind is like trying to build a house without mortar. Let us be quite clear about this – *self-knowledge does not bring self-integration. However, self-surrender does.* A psychiatrist who found Christ said, "The method of trying to change ourselves through the mind without first letting Christ have our spirits is like trying to lift ourselves by tugging at our shoelaces. When we surrender to God, we rise out of the swamps of self-despair as if by magic. Not self-knowledge, but God-knowledge, lifts me out of what I am, to what I want to be."

## Say "Yes"

So we must be quite clear that the transforming action of the mind cannot take place until there has first taken place a transformation in the spirit, only then are we free to turn our attention to the development of right mental attitudes. Once the centre of our personalities has been handed over to God, we can begin to work on the cultivation of thought processes that are in harmony with the Scriptures. *What happens if we try to cultivate an unsurrendered self?* It's like sitting on a box, the lid of which is constantly being blown off by the explosive force of an unsurrendered and unmastered self which is within. As Proverbs 23:7 says, *"For as he thinks in his heart, so is he"* (NKJ). Someone has put it this way: "You are not what you think you are, but what you think, you are." If you think positive thoughts, you'll be a positive person. If you think weak, negative thoughts, you will be a negative person. A management engineer who takes weak and ailing businesses and puts them back on their feet, says that he always starts by interviewing the executives. He usually discovers (so he claims) that the sick business is the result of sick thinking by the board of management. One of his techniques is to get them used to saying the word, "Yes", making them on some occasions repeat the word a hundred times. We Britishers who operate under a less competitive system than our friends on the other side of the Atlantic may balk at this approach. However, the management consultant has a point, for life is designed to be positive and ongoing and we need to learn how to face it with a high degree of optimism and faith.

## The divine "Yes"

This does not mean, of course, that we must say "Yes" to wrong-doing, for that would be decidedly foolish and unscriptural. We must say "Yes" to all that is creative, positive, purposeful and in harmony with God's will – and "No" to all that is not. A disciple asked his teacher, "What is the one ultimate word of truth?" The teacher replied, "Yes." The disciple asked the question again, and the teacher replied, "Are you deaf?" The ultimate word of truth is "Yes". But not a random "Yes" that links itself to anything that comes along. It should be a "Yes" that is linked to the long-range victory which Jesus Christ alone can achieve. There are many who take up the theme of "Positive Thinking" but they are not quite sure to which ends their positive thinking is tied. The Christian defines his "Yes", and defines it in terms of Jesus Christ. I love to ponder the Moffatt translation of 2 Corinthians 1:20: "The divine 'yes' has at last sounded in him, for in him is the 'yes' that affirms all the promises of God." Men and women were not able to say a meaningful "Yes" to life until they saw it revealed to them through the incarnation of Jesus. When they saw the meaning of life in Him then they could say "Yes" with no inhibitions – or hesitations. When we think, affirm, say and act out the "Yes" of Jesus then life itself becomes a "Yes". You are affirming something which the universe affirms.

## A Renewed Mind

And be renewed in the spirit of your mind. (Ephesians 4:23)

For some, saying "Yes" to life may mean the difference between a creative life and an uncreative one. Go over your vocabulary and eliminate words and thoughts such as "I am worried sick", "I'm afraid of that" and "I can't do it". Under this sick thinking, it won't be long before your whole person turns sick. A teacher once told me she had lost her job for the third time because of self-condemnation. She said, "I continually wonder whether I have sinned here or there, until it becomes an obsession with me. My whole problem is my relationship with God." I said to her, "No, that's not your problem. Your problem is not so much your relationship with God, but rather your relationship with yourself." God is always ready to forgive our sins once they are confessed and brought out, but even He is hindered from renewing a person's life when that person refuses to accept God's "Yes" and continues to live by a "No". Just as you cannot live by denying yourself food, so you cannot live spiritually or psychologically on a "No". It must be a "Yes". Learn to be a "Yes" person in the fullest sense of the word, by positively accepting all that God wants to do in you and through you, by the Person of His Son. When you say "Yes" to Jesus you are affirming something which the universe affirms and echoing something which the whole of creation echoes. In Christ, life is good, creative and open-ended. Say "Yes" – and start linking yourself with the creative purposes of God as expressed through Jesus Christ.

## Put on the Lord Jesus

In Philippians 4:8 the apostle Paul asks us to keep in mind "whatever is true, whatever is noble, whatever is right, whatever is pure, whatever is lovely, whatever is admirable – if anything is excellent or praiseworthy". No wonder he finishes by saying, "And the God of peace will be with you" (v.9). He could have said, "Keep in mind the critical, the negative, the unlovely, the impure the obscene – and the devils of conflict and unhappiness will be with you." I once read about a woman who went travelling for the first time in the hills of North India. She went to bed with the thought of tigers and leopards in her mind and during the night she awoke with a start to see two eyes glowing at her from the other side of the room. Her shrieks brought her friends running – only to discover that the two glowing eyes were nothing more than glow-worms. The negative person is always turning glow-worms into tigers. The Christian position is found in Romans 13:14: "Put on the Lord Jesus Christ, and make no provision for the flesh ..." (NKJ). In other words, make no provision in your thinking for the flesh to get the upper hand. If you think you will fall – you will. You have already fallen in thought. "Expect victory and you will have victory. Expect defeat and you will have defeat, for you are already defeated in mind." In putting on the Lord Jesus Christ, affirming His affirmations, living in His strength and power, you affirm Affirmation, promising yourself what He promises you and realising true Reality.

## Cosmic backing

In considering the importance of the mind and affirming the great affirmations of Scripture, sometimes people say: *Is not this merely autosuggestion?* No, it is far deeper than that. In autosuggestion, we can suggest things to ourselves that may not be in accordance with the facts of the universe, but when we affirm what we know God wishes for us, then our thinking has cosmic backing. Let's take a few positive steps that will help us move towards a more affirmative lifestyle.

1. *Stand off from your life and decide what kind of person you are.* Which way do you view life? Positively or negatively? Do you look out through eyes of fear or through eyes of faith? Are you a pessimist or an optimist?

2. *Surrender your negative attitudes to God.* Don't spit on both hands and say, I'm going to fight this negative attitude that I have, for that will make you tense and strained. Ask God to take it over – with your consent and co-operation.

3. *Now decide to be God's "Yes-man".* Accept the resources of God and begin to live on His "Yes". Say "Yes" to God's "Yes". Realise that all God accomplished through Jesus, He wants to accomplish through you. And the same power that was available to Him is available to you.

4. *Go over your vocabulary and prune all your negative thoughts and phrases.* You will need to ask God's help to accomplish this, as they become grooved in your mind. But once the basic attitude is reversed and you become a "Yes" person instead of a "No" person, then they will drop off like the leaves in the autumn wind.

5. *Spend time in prayer, and the reading of the Scriptures so as to expose yourself to God's "Yes's".* In meditating upon the Scriptures, gather up those marvellous statements and verses such as Romans 12:2: "Do not conform any longer to the pattern of this world, but be transformed by the renewing of your mind. Then you will be able to test and approve what God's will is – his good, pleasing and perfect will." Use them, and let them drop into your mind hour by hour, until they become your habitual thoughts. Remember God has not only spoken in His Word, the Bible; He speaks through it still. The creative God still creates and, from His Word, He will bring forth "treasures new and old". (The CWR publication, *Getting the Best from the Bible* is a useful tool for biblical meditation.)

The whole purpose of a renewed mind is, of course, so that "we might be able to make out what the will of God is" (Rom. 12:2, Moffatt). This is the central purpose of transformation – the linking of your mind with the mind of God. When your mind and God's mind come together, then everything, both in heaven and earth, fall into place. You will then discover that the will of God is "good" – good for you; "acceptable" – life accepts it, recognising that this is the purpose for which it was made; "perfect" – God's goal for everything. The steps are quite simple: we soak our minds in Scripture so that we learn to think as God thinks. We discover, as we do this, that thinking God's thoughts leads us to do His will, and doing His will is the purpose for which we were created – it's "good" for us. The "good" is confirmed by the universe around and life turns out to be perfect.

# 6

# **Redeemed**
# emotions

*"The feelings or emotions are the driving forces of the soul ..."*

N ow that we have examined the transformation of the mind, we turn to consider the transformation of the emotions. Some Christians give a good deal of attention to having a transformed mind, while failing to see the need for transformed emotions, and thus the transformed mind is cancelled out by the untransformed emotions. The emotions have been called "the driving force of the personality" and if they are allowed to drive the life in wrong or contrary directions then the personality becomes a battleground, instead of a healthy co-ordinated whole.

What is an emotion? William James defines it as "the state of mind that manifests itself in sensible change in the body". So emotions do not merely influence the body; they can produce noticeable changes too. The change does not take place in just one part of the body. Our emotions affect every single cell of the body, down to the marrow in our bones – for good or ill. It is difficult to separate thought from emotion, of course, for almost every thought has an emotional tone. Some say we "think with our emotions" for the mind often gathers reasons to justify the emotions. A mind filled with wrong or negative emotional attitudes is unable to think straight for the emotions twist the thinking. So to think straight we have to become emotionally straight. A doctor said, "If wrong thinking has slain its thousands then wrong emotions have slain their ten thousands." Emotions then are important, and the God who made them has in His infinite wisdom provided also for their redemption and redirection.

## "The jealous husband's test"

We must make clear, right at the start, that emotions are a wonderful endowment to our personalities – when directed toward the right ends. Someone has said, "The feelings or emotions are the driving forces of the soul. If properly harnessed they can drive you to great goals; if unharnessed they can drive you 'nuts'." I once read about a man who was carried into hospital with an extremely high heart beat, constant vomiting and excessive perspiration. He had never been sick in his life, but one morning he had walked into his daughter's bedroom to discover that his wife had killed her – his only daughter – and then committed suicide. Immediately those physical symptoms manifested themselves. The organs in his body were structurally the same as they were an hour before he discovered the tragic scene, but now, functionally, they were different. One moment they functioned in health – the next they functioned in ill-health. The emotions made the difference. The power of the emotions is seen in the test given to a woman in the days of Moses, as described in Numbers 5:11–24. If a woman was suspected of immorality, she was taken to the priest and was given dirty water to drink. If guilty, she would have pains. If not guilty, there would be no pain. The emotion of guilt produced those pains. Emotional upsets result in functional disturbances.

## Emotional blood pressure

Michael de Montaigne tells a story of a man he knew who persuaded his dinner guests that they had just eaten a baked cat. A young woman immediately began to vomit and, not long afterwards, fell into a coma and died. Her emotions caused a functional disturbance in otherwise healthy organs. One doctor claims that most people who have headaches, in which the pain goes down into the cords of the neck, have them because of emotional issues. There is nothing wrong with the nerves, but the messages being sent along them are fearful and shot through with anxiety. John Schindler claims that anxious people who have pains that seem like ulcer pains may have no ulcer. The mind sends messages of fear, stress and conflict to the stomach which, in turn, produces the pains. Another doctor claims that a great deal of high blood pressure comes from the emotions and that most people with high blood pressure, when under an anaesthetic, show normal readings. The pressure is in the emotions. Many people get up in the morning feeling as if they had not been to bed. And why? Some emotion is setting up tension in the subconscious mind, and the subconscious mind is operating in fear even though the conscious mind is asleep. It's like driving a car with the brakes on. The facts are too many to try and escape. We must get our emotions straightened out if we are going to be straightened out.

## Made for truth

It is only when we understand the strength of the emotions that we will be motivated to seek God for their spiritual transformation. A woman, in describing a row she had had with her husband, said, "The next day I asked him for a divorce. No answer. Now I am flippant. I put on a false front of flippancy, but I can't sleep and my stomach is tied in knots." You cannot lie to yourself for you are not made for lies – you are made for truth. The subconscious mind sees through all subterfuges and records the fact that deep down there is conflict. Some years ago the *British Medical Journal* contained these lines:

> Eat all kind Nature can bestow,
> It will amalgamate down below
> If the mind says so!
> But once you begin to doubt
> Your gastric juices will find it out!

A pastor confided to a Christian counsellor that, during the days of his courtship, whenever he was with his fiancée, he would lose his previous meal. Once he asked her to marry him, and she agreed, his digestion was quite normal. The uncertainty of whether or not she would agree to marriage affected his ability to digest his food. Since our emotions can upset us, we should make sure that the messages they send to our bodies are ones of confidence and faith. Whether we like it or not we are made in the likeness of our emotions.

## God's design for the emotions

We now ask ourselves the question: *What steps can we take to have our emotions transformed?*

The first step we must take is to see that there is a basic cause for our wrong emotions and that *what was caused can be cured*. Our emotional development begins at birth, perhaps even prior to birth. As we begin to develop and grow we learn how to trust or not to trust. We experience fear, anger, jealousy, sadness, joy, elation, happiness and other emotional reactions. Our emotions grow and develop in different ways. One person may develop a balanced emotional life; another an unbalanced one. Our emotions are a gift from God and, when He created us, He created us as emotional beings. However, since Adam's transgression in the Garden of Eden, a curse has fallen upon all of mankind and we do not function in the way God originally intended and designed. Christ's death on the cross has opened a way whereby God can bring about great changes within our personality. His goal is to bring us to the place where we think as He thinks, feel as He feels and will as He wills. The goal God has set for our emotional make-up is that described for us in this beautiful passage in Galatians chapter 5: "But the fruit of the Spirit is love, joy, peace, patience, kindness, goodness, faithfulness, gentleness and self-control" (vv.22–23). Whatever damage has been done to your emotions through childhood experiences or traumatic events, God can sweep into your life with His healing power and touch those raw and sensitive emotions so that they work in His way – for Him and not against Him.

## Learned behaviour

Although God is both eager and ready to heal the emotions that have been damaged by past relationships, we must see that we also have a personal responsibility in this matter. Most Christians, I find, blind their eyes to this point, but until it is faced and dealt with, there can be no true healing. So before we can receive the emotional healing God wants to give us, *we must accept our share of the problem*. For example, when we were shown hate in our early years, how did we respond? Was it not by hating back? When anger was displayed towards us, did we not reciprocate in the same manner? As the garment of our lives began to take shape on the loom of the developmental years – when the shuttle of hate, anger and criticism was passed through to us – did we not pass it back with an equal amount of hatred and anger? We were not just faced with bitterness and hatred; we *learned* it. It is for this reason I say that no complete healing of damaged emotions can come about, in any Christian's heart, until that person has learned to accept some personal responsibility for harbouring hatred, resentment and bitterness in his or her heart. The responsibility goes further than acknowledging the hatred – we must get rid of it in an act of repentance and confession; first to God and then to all those against whom we have aimed our hatred and contempt.

The damaged emotions inside you are not part of God's purposes for you. God wills their removal. When God and you both will they should be straightened out, they will be.

## Guided – to great goals

We now need to focus on some final steps in our discussions on the transformation of the emotions. We have said that *our first step is to recognise that what was caused can be cured. The second step is to accept our share of the blame.* Now the third – *don't deny any wrong emotions and pretend they are not there.* This will only drive them into the subconscious where they will work havoc. If you feel angry don't say, "I am not angry," but admit it to yourself, and face it. Once it is faced then you can do something about it. There are four ways to deal with anger. You can repress it, suppress it, express it or confess it. The Bible way is that of confession. If you are angry with God, tell Him so and ask His forgiveness. If you are angry with another person don't say, "You make me so angry." Say, "I am angry – please forgive me." The fourth step is this – *cultivate the opposite emotions to the ones which have hurt and hindered you.* If the wrong emotion has been fear, then cultivate faith. Read all the scriptures you can on faith, for what you read in the Bible will pass into your emotions, and re-create a new emotional spectrum. If a wrong emotion has been hatred, then cultivate love. Read and meditate on 1 Corinthians 13 until it infiltrates your whole personality. If it has been self-hate, then love yourself in God. Your emotions, when you bring God into them through prayer and meditation in His Word, work with you, not against you. Let those transformed emotions drive you to great goals.

# 7

# A **healthy** body

*"Jesus is more interested in us being well than the most sincere and enthusiastic family doctor."*

We now focus our attention on the transformation of the body. This immediately raises the question: *Does the life of God within our souls and spirits affect the physical to any great degree?* It does. God wills health, for salvation is wholeness – wholeness to the total person, including the body. This is not to say that God does not use physical sickness and affliction to advance His purposes, where otherwise those purposes could not be achieved, but He must never be looked upon as the Author of illness. The whole tenor of Scripture proclaims that God is interested in the physical as well as the spiritual health of His children. It must be said right away, however, that Christianity is not a healing cult, for its primary purpose is not to keep our bodies in repair, but to develop our spiritual relationship with our Father in heaven and to prepare us for eternity. The ultimate aim of the Christian faith is not merely to make us either happy or healthy – but holy. *Health and happiness are by-products of holiness.* If we seek health first, it will evade us. If we seek happiness first, it will evade us. But if we seek first the kingdom of God and His righteousness, then all these things will be added unto us (Matt. 6:31–34). Let us make absolutely certain, before we begin to investigate this subject, that we place the emphasis where God places it – on Him, not on health.

## Jesus' attitude towards sickness

What was the attitude of the Lord Jesus Christ towards sickness and disease during His time here on earth? When we examine the record of the Gospels, we discover that one of the reasons why He came to this world was to show us what God is really like, and He accomplished this by healing men and women of their sicknesses and diseases. At the beginning of His ministry He declared an all-out offensive against sin, disease and death.

In Luke 4:39 we read,

"So he bent over her and rebuked the fever, and it left her ..."

He rebuked the fever in the same way that He rebuked demons. He saw both sin and sickness in the same light – evil forces and intruders in His Father's world. Someone has said that, whenever we meet Jesus Christ in the Gospels, He is either healing someone, on His way to heal someone, or coming back from healing someone. Practically speaking, Jesus' attitude towards sickness in the Gospels was that of any good doctor today – *he fought it all the way*. Nowhere in the Gospels do we ever discover a hint of retreat or compromise over His position concerning sickness and disease. He never refused to heal anyone who came to Him for help, and reproved any suggestion of His unwillingness or inability to heal (Luke 5:12–13; Mark 9:23). One third of His ministry was taken up with the healing of the sick and not once did He ever pray concerning this matter, "If it be thy will". We will probably take our greatest step forward towards physical health when we realise that Jesus is more interested in us being well than even the most sincere and enthusiastic family doctor.

## The unchanging Christ

Clearly it was Jesus' desire that the people of His day should be delivered from their sicknesses and afflictions. Not once did He ever say that sickness was a blessing. Someone has pointed out (although too much must not be made of it) that whilst there is a Beatitude for those who suffer persecution, there is no Beatitude for those who suffer physically. What was Jesus' strategy for helping people be free of sickness? He said that faith in His Father's willingness and ability to give His children good gifts was the key. His motive in healing was not simply to produce proof of His divinity (although this is evident to some degree) but rather because His great heart was moved to compassion at the sight of those who were sick and suffering. *Jesus did not heal people to prove He was God; He healed them because He was God.* The word "compassion" is used over and over again to describe His motivation for healing the sick. This was the main reason why He went out of His way to heal those who had neither asked Him nor thought of doing so. He rejoiced in straightening bent and broken limbs. He *delighted in* unstopping deaf ears, opening blind eyes and making the lame leap with joy. Jesus healed because the love of God, flowing irresistibly through Him in a torrent of compassion, simply swept evil and ill-health away as the debris that it is. Make no mistake about it – this is His attitude today.

## The door to health

One of the questions often troubling people in seeking healing for their bodies is this – *Does the atonement of Christ cover our physical as well as our spiritual needs?* There are obvious differences between the spiritual and the physical of course but, in general, God has accepted the challenge which the twin evils of the human race (sin and sickness) produced in His universe, and has fully met it at the cross. There He took on Himself everything that would and does fall upon us, and suffered with us and for us. One writer put it most beautifully when he wrote, "There [at the cross] the world's sin and suffering were forced through the channel of a single Heart." Some Christians feel that Isaiah 53:4 applies only to spiritual healing and has nothing whatever to do with our physical afflictions. The fact that Jesus partly fulfilled this prophecy when He healed the sick, is made clear by Matthew when he writes: "This was to fulfil what was spoken through the prophet Isaiah:

"He took up our infirmities and carried our diseases"
(Matt. 8:17).

As Matthew saw the sick threading their way to Christ for healing, he was inspired by the Holy Spirit to relate the scene to Isaiah's prediction, which had been given centuries before. Healing of the body is an integral part of Christ's sacrifice on the cross and through it He has provided an open door of release from the sicknesses and infirmities of life. We must learn to walk through that door into the radiant health which Christ can provide.

## God – a Mother and a Father

The following two texts express quite clearly the masculine and feminine characteristics that are to be found in God:

"Can a mother forget the baby at her breast ...?
Though she may forget,
I will not forget you!" (Isa. 49:15)

"... how much more will your Father in heaven give the Holy Spirit to those who ask him!" (Luke 11:13)

God's love we are told surpasses that of an earthly father and mother. The marvellous revelation of the New Testament is that God *in Christ* is no longer the unapproachable One of Sinai, but has become a Man – like us, in everything except sin. The mission of Jesus was to share our sufferings and sorrows, then transform them into a new life for the healing of spirit, soul and body. The inspiration God in Christ brought into this world has encouraged men and women to build hospitals, establish clinics and to travel the world with the message that God really cares. Only non-Christian religions let people die on the streets, believing it to be the will of God that they suffer their afflictions in silence. The Christian gospel reaches out to bring healing in every way possible (through prayer, medicine, surgery, etc.) based on the assumption that it is God's will that we combat sickness and disease in every way possible. Those who teach that sickness and suffering are placed upon us by God, produce in their hearers a kind of spiritual schizophrenia. On the one hand, they see doctors and nurses tirelessly giving themselves to the work of healing the sick while they, themselves, are taught that God is the Author of it. If sickness is the will of God then no doctor, however skilled, can ever hope to remove it.

## Blocks to healing

There are many reasons why people are not healed and I want to deal with the two major ones – *a false view of God, and a subconscious desire to remain sick for attention-getting purposes.* Some people, because of deep emotional damage in their developmental years, have a false view of God, which is drawn largely from a poor image of their parents or foster parents and other significant adults with whom they had a close relationship. They view God as someone who is intent on punishing them and this punitive image of God encourages them to hold on to their sickness as a form of self-punishment. The conditioning a child receives, in a bad parent–child relationship, is often responsible for that child, when an adult, being unable to accept the blessings of health in the way God delights to give, They simply cannot conceive of a God who is good enough to give them health, and thus they fail to reach out and receive from His hand the blessings He so graciously offers. This unconscious resistance and inability to receive, can sometimes block the healing power of God from flowing into that person's body. Such a person needs to look long at the picture of God as presented by His Son, the Lord Jesus Christ, such as in Luke 11:1–13: " 'If you then, though you are evil, know how to give good gifts to your children, how much more will your Father in heaven give the Holy Spirit to those who ask him!' " (v.13). God is a Father who *cares* for His children, and longs that they might experience, and enjoy, the abundance of His provisions, which includes not only peace for the soul, but life for the body.

## Facing reality

Another reason why some people stay unhealed *is because they subconsciously use their sickness as an attention-getting device*. The human mind is so devious that, when it feels the personality is not receiving the love it needs to function properly, it will settle for the next best thing – attention. And sickness is an almost sure way of getting it. This is why, whenever we find ourselves gripped by a sickness that stubbornly refuses to leave, we should explore this possibility and ask ourselves: *Do I really want to be well?* Was the man in John 5:1–9 in this condition? I don't really know, but it looks as if Jesus wanted to raise the possibility: "Jesus ... asked him, 'Do you want to get well?'" (v.6). Alongside the possibility that we can use our sickness as a subconscious device to get attention, there is also another side to this – *using sickness as a form of escapism*. A woman in a church I once pastored, developed a sickness which the doctors diagnosed as psychosomatic. They told her, "There is nothing structurally wrong with you – you can get better whenever you wish." This so shocked her that she asked my help in getting to the bottom of her problem. We discovered a deep inner conflict that, whenever she was approached by a young man who showed a romantic interest in her, her subconscious reasoned thus – if you get married what will happen to mother? So, to keep her suitors away her subconscious provided her with a good excuse – sickness. She surrendered the whole matter to God, and instantly recovered. It is sometimes easier to face sickness than to face the reality that remains if the sickness is not there.

# Right
# **relationships**

*"The law of life, from the tiniest cell upwards, is based on the fact that each entity must lose its life in order to find it again."*

Now that we have seen the possibility of being transformed in spirit, in mind, in the emotions and in the body, we must experience the *transformation of our relationships*. Someone has said that the Christian demand is twofold – unreservedly given to God and unbreakably given to each other. "A double surrender" is, therefore, imperative – to God and to the fellowship of His Church. Many reasons have been suggested by preachers and teachers for Peter's downfall and collapse when he denied his Lord (Matt 26:26–35). The usual one put forward is that, "he followed afar off" and, therefore, the distance he put between himself and his Lord was responsible for his disloyalty. Dr. E. Stanley Jones suggests a deeper reason. He claims the truth is seen in the attitude Peter displayed when he said, "If everyone else deserts you, I won't" (Matt. 26:33, TLB). The words "everyone else" are crucial. Inwardly he had pulled out of the fellowship and instead of being in a "we" relationship, he was in a "they – I" relationship.

He was, therefore, superior and critical, self-righteous and aloof. He broke with the fellowship and automatically broke with Jesus. Many are ready to give themselves to God for inward transformation, but they are not ready to give themselves to the fellowship of His Church and be transformed in their relationships with others. They say, "I can't give myself to these weak, spineless people." So they stand away, superior, aloof and only partly transformed.

## The "we – I" relationship

We catch another glimpse of the attitude of Peter in Ezekiel 3:14–21. When Ezekiel went to speak to the captives by the river, the scripture says, "I went in bitterness and in the anger of my spirit, with the strong hand of the Lord upon me." He was all set to rebuke them for their sins. It was a "they – I" relationship. Then God invited him to sit "where they sat" (v.15, NKJ), and Ezekiel said, "I sat among them, overwhelmed, for seven days" (v.15b, TLB). When he "sat where they sat", and learned to sympathise and empathise, the relationship changed from "they – I" to "we". God let him speak for them when the seven days were up, and when he spoke he spoke with power. No one earns the right to speak for others until he has identified himself with them in a "we" relationship, and the central message of Christianity is just such a relationship. In Old Testament times, the relationship of God to men was essentially a "they – I" one. God commanded, and they were expected to obey. It was the age of the law. But then Jesus came and God literally sat where we sat. He identified Himself with us until at the cross the identification became complete and He took upon Himself our sins – "became sin for us". There the "I" merged into the "we" – completely and eternally. Since the centre of the Christian faith is a "we" relationship, then our relationships must be on that basis too. We relate to others not through law, but through love.

## "Is it 'we' or is it 'I'?"

Earlier we suggested that the reason why Peter denied his Lord was due to his inward attitudes of "they – I". Now look at him after Pentecost. Having repented bitterly for his withdrawal and disloyalty, he is now filled with the Holy Spirit. Notice the change in his language. "We are all witnesses" (Acts 2:32). "Why do you stare on us as if by our own power or godliness we had made this man walk?" (Acts 3:12). Trace his statements through the book of Acts (and also through his two epistles) and you will discover that, after Pentecost, this man passed from a sub-Christian to a fully Christian relationship – which is fellowship. Since God made us for relationships, one of the most eventful things that can happen to us is to experience transformation in this area. A psychologist said, "The disease of the world is the disease of the individual personality." If a person tries to live out life on this earth in a "they – I" attitude then the person will experience great difficulties in his or her relationships. Dr W.E. Sangster tells the story of a boy who pumped the organ every Sunday in a certain church. Once after a special service, the little boy came out from behind the curtain and said to the organist, "We played well today, sir, didn't we?" The organist, in disdain, said, "Well, I played well." The next Sunday, when the organist sat down to play, there was no sound. The organist was nonplussed. Then a voice came from behind the curtain, "Now is it 'we' or is it 'I'?"

## "All men 'cremated' equal"

The law of life, from the tiniest cell upward, is based on the fact that each entity must lose its life in order to find it again. "Whoever loses his life for my sake will find it" (Matt. 16:25, NKJ). We are told that each cell when it starts out is capable of being the whole organism. However, it surrenders to the organism. It takes a particular place, serves the rest and discovers its exact place in the fellowship of the whole. It is the law of self-surrender at work.

When that law is broken then a serious disturbance is created within the organism. A doctor described cancer as, "a group of cells turned selfish". They stubbornly refuse to serve the rest of the organism, insist on being independent and demand that the rest of the organism serves them. They attempt to save their lives and instead lose them – they eat their way to their own destruction. A cell that loses its life for the sake of the others becomes contributive. A cell that saves its own life becomes cancerous. If every member of Christ's body would only say "we" instead of "they – I" we would have the solution to many of our problems. Our scientists are saying the same thing to the world at large. If we don't say "we" in international affairs then, they claim, the world of Kaye Phelps will come true:

Let not the atom bomb
Be the final sequel
In which all men
Are cremated equal.
Our model for unity

One of the biggest hindrances to the "we" relationship in the Church of Jesus Christ is our *denominationalism*. It is not so much the fact that we have different denominations (that in itself is bad enough), but more the attitude that sets us in a "they – I" relationship. Although, thank God, things are changing in this direction, there are still far too many churches who co-operate with one another in this framework. It is time we said "we". The kind of relationship which God wants amongst His children is the one that exists between Jesus and His Father, and the one for which He prayed, "... that all of them may be one, Father, just as you are in me and I am in you. May they also be in us so that the world may believe that you have sent me" (John 17:21). Jesus prayed that our relationship might be like the one He enjoyed with His Father – that is, true unity. One American writer claims that there is nothing stopping all true Christian churches from having a union such as Christ enjoys with His Father – an organic union with a federal structure. He points out that, although the Father and the Son were one, each had a distinctive name and personality. On this basis he claims, "the churches can get together tomorrow". I do not believe (as do some) that the outside world is put off by the many denominations. What does hinder it is the lack of love and unity that exists between us. A drinking fountain I once saw in America, had a hundred different jets of water, but all coming from one source. If the Church were more like this, the world would drink of such a fountain!

## "Come to the cross"

In considering this question of the transformation of our relationships, we must see that Christian love and concern ought to be demonstrated not only to those within the fellowship of the Church but those outside of it also. Someone has said that, "the transformation of a Christian is not completed until the evangelised become evangelists". A transformed personality – transformed by Christ, that is – will want to reach out to those whose lives are untouched by Jesus Christ. I once read about a businessman, a butcher, who was awakened by the verse, "The Spirit and the bride say, 'Come'" (Rev. 22:17). He said to himself: "Why, I've been a hearer all my life, and have never said to anybody 'Come'. My business is good. It only needs me four hours a day, so the rest I will give to God for the express task of bringing others into His Church." He went to his pastor and said, "Give me a job?" The pastor replied, "Here's a list of people in this city who ought to be Christians and are not; see what you can do with them."

That man, who couldn't stand in a pulpit and make a speech, was responsible, in two years, for five hundred people coming to Christ. Before he began this work he had a bad heart. He forgot about his bad heart and it settled down to normal. He surprised himself. You too can surprise yourself when you allow God to transform you from the "they – I" relationship to the one that puts an arm around a sinner and says, "I am not better than you, but I know the way to the cross. Let's walk together to Calvary."

## The point of interest

The human mind is adept at finding reasons why we should not go out of our way to share the love and compassion of Christ with those who do not know Him. I once heard a preacher speak on "The Woman at the Well". He gave a list of reasons why Jesus should not have spoken to the woman. Here they are:

1. She was a woman.

2. She was a woman alone.

3. She was a bad woman.

4. She was a bad woman, alone.

5. She was a Samaritan.

6. She came from Sychar, which literally means "drunken", assumed to be taken from the character of the inhabitants.

7. He was tired.

8. It was noon, and probably very hot.

Then, in finishing his sermon, he gave the two reasons why Jesus overcame these barriers: a) her need and b) God's will – "the will of him who sent me".

Those two factors still lay claim upon us today. Everyone needs salvation and God wills it. The "will" is for everybody and the "need" includes everybody. A famous evangelist said he continually affirms to himself, "God wills it, man needs it – I'll do it." While there are many things that could be said about the Samaritan woman, I want to point out just one thing in this story that might help you share your faith with others. Look at how Jesus opened the conversation. He began at the point of her interest –

with the thing she came for – "water" and then went from water to "living water". When you show an interest in what others are interested in, they tend to respond more readily and be interested in what you are interested in.

# **Transformation**
## through right values

*"If we don't surrender the material to God, then it will not be long before God is pushed out by the material."*

The last, and by no means least, area we must tackle is that of the transformation of our material values. If we don't transform the material into the image of the spiritual, then the material will transform us into its own image. Some Christians allow material things to gain the upper hand. Instead of serving God with mammon, they make mammon their god, and soon they begin to look like their god – cold and metallic. The light of love fades from their eyes and, although being made a living soul, they become only living flesh. With Edna St Vincent Millay they say:

> I cannot tell what loves have come and gone,
> I only know that summer sang in me
> A little while, and in me sings no more.

The winter of materialism sets in and as multitudes of Christians have discovered it is a frosty experience in the soul. A story is told of a leopard who was shot and his skin made into a coat, which was hung in a shop window with a price mark of £500. His family, out walking, stopped at the window and, recognising the skin of their father, said, "He was better off when he wasn't worth so much. At least he was alive!" Many pursue material things only to discover, when they have gained them, that an inner deadness takes over. When we make acquisition our god, we find that instead of us owning it – it owns us. Mammon can become either our master or a message. You must decide which one it is to be. If dedicated to God, it is a message. When unsurrendered, it is a master – and what a master! This aspect of surrender is the turntable on which life turns from the material to the spiritual. If we don't surrender the material to God, then it will not be long before God is pushed out by the material. The question we must ask ourselves is this; *Who owns my posssessions; God or me?* A Christian is not a proprietor of his possessions, but a steward; surrendering them to God does more than settle a material issue – it determines our life-attitude. We become men and women under orders. It transforms the secular into the sacred. It turns wealth into a witness. It makes money become a message. One pastor I heard of referred to the weekly collection in his church as "an offering of minted personality". Our text today shows us that, just as some are called to the ministry of preaching, so others are called to make money for God. Ledgers must be handled with the same sense of mission and sacredness as a Bible in a pulpit. Howard Lowry has defined religion like this: "It conceives of all man does as a calling, and of his life as a piece, a unity of richly component parts." Notice that he says, "of all man does as a calling". We are each called to different tasks and we must find God's plan for our lives and work that plan. When we do, we become creators working under the Creator.

## The final transformation

A major emphasis in this book has been upon the fact that all of life is based on transformation. We are transformed either upwards or downwards depending on which side of life we stand – God's or the devil's. For those of us who have received Jesus Christ into our lives, we are able, in His Name, to transform everything we touch. And why is this? Because God transformed Himself into man, became like us, so that we might become like Him. 1 John 3:2b introduces us to the breathtaking fact that the final goal of transformation is to make us like Christ: "What we are to be is not apparent yet, but we do know that when he appears we are to be like him" (Moffatt). Just think of it! We, who are born of the dust, are being gradually transformed into the most beautiful image this planet has ever seen – the image of Christ. This road, which takes us from "glory to glory" will lead us eventually to the final goal of being transformed into the perfect image of Christ. We are to be with Him and like Him for ever and ever. It was said of a blacksmith, in New England, USA, that he lived so much in thought with the essayist Emerson that he looked like him. We, who love the Lord Jesus Christ, who daily walk in His light and delight in His truth, will one day *see* Him, and the sight of Him will be so breathtaking, so positively absorbing, that we shall suddenly become like Him, not only in thought, *but in appearance*. This is the final consummation. This is the final transformation.

# National Distributors

**UK (and countries not listed below)**
CWR, PO Box 230, Farnham, Surrey GU9 8EP.
Tel: (01252) 784710 Outside UK (44) 1252 784710

**AUSTRALIA**: CMC Australasia, PO Box 519, Belmont, Victoria 3216.
Tel: (03) 5241 3288

**CANADA**: CMC Distribution Ltd., PO Box 7000, Niagara on the Lake,
Ontario LoS 1JO.
Tel: (0800) 325 1297

**GHANA**: Challenge Enterprises of Ghana, PO Box 5723, Accra.
Tel: (021) 222437/223249 Fax: (021) 226227

**HONG KONG**: Cross Communications Ltd, 1/F, 562A Nathan Road,
Kowloon.
Tel: 2780 1188 Fax: 2770 6229

**INDIA**: Crystal Communications, 10-3-18/4/1, East Marredpally,
Secunderabad – 500 026.
Tel/Fax: (040) 7732801

**KENYA**: Keswick Bookshop, PO Box 10242, Nairobi.
Tel: (02) 331692/226047

**MALAYSIA**: Salvation Book Centre (M) Sdn Bhd, 23 Jalan SS 2/64,
47300 Petaling Jaya, Selangor.
Tel: (03) 78766411/78766797 Fax: (03) 78757066/78756360

**NEW ZEALAND**: CMC New Zealand Ltd, Private Bag, 17910 Green
Lane, Auckland.
Tel: (09) 5249393 Fax: (09) 5222137

**NIGERIA**: FBFM, Helen Baugh House, 96 St Finbarr's College Road, Akoka, Lagos.
Tel: (01) 7747429/4700218/825775/827264

**PHILIPPINES**: OMF Literature Inc, 776 Boni Avenue, Mandaluyong City.
Tel: (02) 531 2183 Fax: (02) 531 1960

**REPUBLIC OF IRELAND**: Scripture Union, 40 Talbot Street, Dublin 1.
Tel: (01) 8363764

**SINGAPORE**: Campus Crusade Asia Ltd, 315 Outram Road, 06–08 Tan Boon Liat Building, Singapore 169074.
Tel: (065) 222 3640

**SOUTH AFRICA**: Struik Christian Books, 80 MacKenzie Street, PO Box 1144, Cape Town 8000.
Tel: (021) 462 4360 Fax: (021) 461 3612

**SRI LANKA**: Christombu Books, 27 Hospital Street, Colombo 1.
Tel: (01) 433142/328909

**TANZANIA**: CLC Christian Book Centre, PO Box 1384, Mkwepu Street, Dar es Salaam.
Tel: (051) 2119439

**UGANDA**: New Day Bookshop, PO Box 2021, Kampala.
Tel: (041) 255377

**ZIMBABWE**: Word of Life Books, Shop 4, Memorial Building, 35 S Machel Avenue, Harare.
Tel: (04) 781305 Fax: (04) 774739

For e-mail addresses, visit the CWR web site: www.cwr.org.uk

# The Discipleship Series

The *Discipleship Series* combines practical advice with biblical principles. Each dynamic title considers some of the most vital aspects of Christian living such as marriage, prayer and the Church. Essential reading!

- *8 Ways to Deepen Your Faith*

  Realise the power of faith and release a new vibrant stride into your Christian walk.

  ISBN: 1–85345–215–7

- *15 Keys to Enjoying the Presence of God*

  Discover how to increase, enhance and understand the sense of God's presence in your life.

  ISBN: 1–85345–210–6

■ £3.99 each

■ *5 Insights to Discovering Your Place in the Body of Christ*

ISBN 1–85345–175–4

- Understanding the gifts in Scripture
- Discovering your ministry
- Developing your gift

■ *10 Principles for a Happy Marriage*

ISBN: 1–85345–173–8

- Engaging approach to marriage God's way
- Healthy marriage check list
- Practical advice and help

■ *15 Ways to a More Effective Prayer Life*

ISBN: 1–85345–174–6

- Revolutionise your prayer life
- Flexible suggestions for the individual
- Considers different personalities and lifestyles

■ £3.99 each

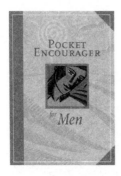

## ■ Pocket Encouragers

This new Pocket Encourager series offers biblical help, guidance and encouragement for everyone.

Each title explores various aspects of the Christian experience, such as relationships, Bible study and coping with responsibility. Great gifts!

■ Pocket Encourager for Men

ISBN: 1–85345–177–0

■ Pocket Encourager for Women

ISBN: 1–85345–178–9

■ Pocket Encourager for Young Adults

ISBN: 1–85345–180–0

■ Pocket Encourager for Leaders

ISBN: 1–85345–179–7

**Available from Christian bookshops or by post from National Distributors**

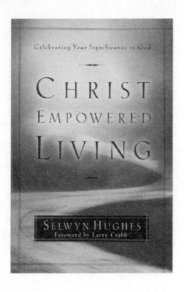

## 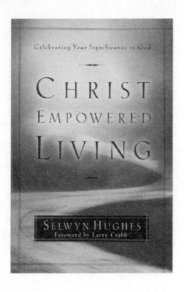 Christ Empowered Living

*Christ Empowered Living* sets out how Christ wants you to live as His follower and how He wants to develop your full spiritual potential. Selwyn delves into the human personality and shows how biblical insights will revolutionise your approach to the way you live and help renew your mind.

■ Chapters include:
- Who Am I?
- Why Do I Do What I Do?
- How Does Change Take Place?
- Monitoring Your Emotional Pulse

■ Hardback

ISBN: 0–8054–2450–4

*"I believe God has been preparing Selwyn for many years, through hardships and joys, through speaking and silence, to write this book … It is a joy to commend this book to a worldwide audience."*
Larry Crabb

*"I always knew I had problems, but I never knew how to fix them. I finally learned how when I attended Christ Empowered Living."*
Scott Hughes, attendee at Christ Empowered Living Seminar.

**Available from Christian bookshops or by post from National Distributors**